M000189358

ELDERSHIP *at the* LORD'S TABLE

ELDERSHIP *at the* LORD'S TABLE

LARA BLACKWOOD PICKREL

CHALICE
P R E S S

ST. LOUIS, MISSOURI

Copyright © 2010 by Lara Blackwood Pickrel.

All rights reserved. For permission to reuse content, please contact Copyright Clearance Center, 222 Rosewood Drive, Danvers, MA 01923, (978) 750-8400, www.copyright.com.

Cover art: Istock Photo
Cover and interior design: Elizabeth Wright

Visit Chalice Press on the World Wide Web at
www.chalicepress.com

10 9 8 7 6 5 4 3 2 1   10 11 12 13 14 15

EPUB: 978-08272-08261   EPDF: 978-08272-08278

Library of Congress Cataloging-in-Publication Data

Pickrel, Lara Blackwood.
  Eldership at the Lord's table / by Lara Blackwood Pickrel.
     p. cm.
  Includes bibliographical references.
   ISBN 978-0-8272-0825-4
 1. Christian Churches (Disciples of Christ)—Doctrines.
2. Lord's Supper—Christian Church (Disciples of Christ) 3.
Elders (Church officers) I. Title.

 BX7321.3.P53 2009
 264'.0663—dc22

                                        2009047367

Printed in the United States of America

Contents

Introduction

Throughout the history of the fellowship that has come to call itself the Christian Church (Disciples of Christ), many a book or pamphlet on the role and ministry of the elder have been written. Some books focus on the history of eldership within the New Testament or our denomination. Others focus on the role of elder as minister. Still others focus exclusively on the provision of sample elders' prayers at the Lord's Table. While this proliferation of resources points to the importance of elders within the church, it also begs the question: Why write yet another resource for elders?

The question, however simple, is a good one. Amidst all of the collective wisdom passed down throughout the history of our denomination, would it not be presumptuous to think that elders need something more to better inform their particular ministry? It might very well be so, and yet I firmly believe that our elders do indeed need more to aid them in their service— particularly their service at the Table. The primary reason for this has everything to do with context.

The development of the Christian Church (Disciples of Christ), as with any other movement, has shifted and changed with each generation of its members.

Although more of this will be examined later in this document, it is safe to say that some aspects of the tradition have carried over through each passing of the torch, while the actual course of the race has brought changes in both belief and practice among the runners. As each generation of Disciples finds themselves in new terrain—hills of new growth, plains of institutional stability, swamplands of cultural battle, and mountains of change—the roles of ministers both lay and ordained have changed. This reality points to the purpose of this pamphlet: to provide Disciples elders of the early twenty-first century with a resource that specifically addresses the role of the elder at the Lord's Table while taking into account our history as a people, our current realities as a church, and our future as a witness of God's grace in the world.

Our fellowship, in the grand scheme of Christian history, is young. And yet, in our short lifetime as a particular people of faith, we have made many contributions to the life of the church universal. Whether large or small, the contributions and achievements of individual Disciples have nearly always been rooted in the experience of the local congregation. Every Hamm, Kinnamon, Jackson, or Watkins started off praising God and learning the meaning(s) of discipleship within a particular church home—this very practical reality points directly to the importance of eldership as ministry in the church.[1] Our corporate

2

witness in the world begins at home. With this thought in mind, I humbly offer up my musings on the role of the Disciples elder at the Lord's Table.

This document can be used in a number of ways. A congregational board of elders may opt to read this work in its entirety over the course of a multiple-week study group. Individual elders may decide to read this booklet as a part of their own personal regimen of study, meditation, and Bible reading. Elders may also choose to peruse the sections of this work that give examples of elders' prayers as they prepare for their service at the Lord's Table. Finally (though not exhaustively), those who have been called to the ministry of eldership may choose to examine the list of resources for elders that can be found at the end of this document so that the wisdom of other Disciples may inform their own ministry to the church. My greatest hope and prayer is that some portion of this resource will be helpful to those men and women who have been called forth to lead and guide this generation of Disciples.

History of Disciples Elders and the Lord's Supper

Many different Christian denominations have some form of office called "elder." However, the history of the eldership within the Christian Church (Disciples of Christ) and the rest of the Stone-Campbell Movement is relatively unique.[2] Because the Stone-Campbell Movement began as a unity movement with a goal of transcending denominational distinctions, various forms of strict ecclesial hierarchy were problematic from the beginning. The way the movement's first leaders chose to move beyond these sectarian forms of ministry was to emphasize the forms of leadership found in the New Testament church: elders/bishops, deacons, and evangelists.[3]

The work of Alexander Campbell clarified the roles of these three types of ministers. While evangelists were charged with evangelism and preaching, and deacons were given roles including property management and visitation, the ministry of the elder was threefold: teaching, shepherding, and guiding the congregation.[4] In this way, most duties that modern Disciples associate

5

with ordained clergy (aside from preaching) were actually a part of the eldership's ministerial portfolio.

This simple order of ministry was important for multiple reasons. First, it was seen as conducive to unity because it was an order taken directly from the Bible rather than any one particular sectarian tradition. Second, it removed the marked distinction between clergy and laity and spread the roles of ministry out among a larger group of people. For many years of our history the ministerial roles and responsibilities have been primarily the calling of the eldership.[5]

Although the Stone-Campbell Movement of the nineteenth century experienced much disagreement on specific meanings of the Lord's Supper as well as who was or was not invited to the Table, they still "established a broad and early consensus that the Lord's Supper was the central act of Christian worship" and should be "observed at least every Sunday."[6] From the beginning, elders took on an important role in the observance of this ordinance. In his resource on Disciples eldership, Peter M. Morgan remarks :

> The most consistent function of elders through-
> out the Disciples history has been as presiders
> at the Lord's Table. In some congregations that
> is the totality of the elders' ministry. It is a rare
> exception when the elders do not administer
> the Lord's Supper. Two things are overseen

by elders at the table. First is the linking of the congregation to its source of life, God made known in Jesus Christ. Second is the proper conduct of the rites of this service of worship.[7]

Though many congregations still exercise the elder's ministerial roles of teaching, shepherding, and guiding within the congregation, most Disciples congregations now put a strong emphasis on the role of the elder at the Table. Because of this focus and because of the importance of the Lord's Supper to Disciples throughout history and geography, we move now to a basic theology of the Table.

Theology of the Lord's Table

If a visitor were to peruse the homepage of the Christian Church (Disciples of Christ), he or she might stumble upon a page titled "About the Disciples." This page contains links to various documents that explain Disciples' symbols, beliefs, and practices, as well as a vision statement and a mission statement. The page has a link to a "Communion" page, which has the following statement:

> The Lord's Supper or Communion is celebrated in weekly worship. It is open to all who are followers of Jesus Christ. The practice of Holy Communion has become the central element of worship within the Disciples tradition.
>
> Disciples' observance of the Lord's Supper emanates from the upper room, where Jesus shared bread and wine with his disciples on the eve of his crucifixion. Through the power of the Holy Spirit, the living Christ is met and received in the sharing of the bread and the cup, representative of the body and blood of Jesus. The presence of the living Lord is affirmed and he is proclaimed to be the dominant power in our lives.[8]

This statement points to two of the primary meanings that Disciples attach to the Lord's Supper: the unity in Christ of all believers as represented by an "open" Table and the invitation and presence of Christ at the Table.

The open Table is a powerful symbol of our unity in Christ, as well as the universality of Christ's invitation to know the love of God. Christian unity has been a fundamental focus of the Disciples from the very beginning of the Stone-Campbell Movement, and the need for it has been expressed powerfully by individuals throughout our history. In 1923, in a book on Christian worship, Peter Ainslie and H. C. Armstrong expressed the importance of unity in this manner:

> The unity of Christendom is as fundamental as the death of Jesus on the Cross and his resurrection from the tomb... When the unity of Christendom ceases to be the message and attitude of the Disciples, we have no moral right of existence.[9]

Such a powerful statement pounds home the importance of unity and also points to two other fundamentals of Disciples belief that present themselves at the Table. For Ainslie, Armstrong, and many other Disciples throughout our history, the cross, the resurrection, and Christian unity are the theological focal points that come together at the Table.

When we speak of the presence of Christ at the Table, Disciples often silently agree to disagree. For some, Christ is actually present during the observance of communion; others see the Lord's Supper purely in terms of remembrance and a memorial of Christ's life, death, and resurrection. These disagreements span back into the very beginning of our history. Campbell, Stone, Richardson, and countless others who helped to birth the Stone-Campbell movement often disagreed on the precise meaning of the Lord's Supper in relation to Christ's presence.[10] What can be said universally in regards to Disciples Table observance is that (in some way, either literal or symbolic or a measure of each) the Lord's Supper gives meaning to the lives of church members in light of the cross, the resurrection, and Christian unity. At the Table we come to understand our lives and ourselves in relation to these three theological concepts, and therefore our prayers at the Table ought to point church members toward a deeper contemplation of those mysteries and realities.

Elders' Prayers at the Table

Disciples celebrate the Lord's Supper in a variety of ways. Sometimes communion takes place before the sermon, while in other congregations it occurs after the sermon. In some churches, the congregation comes forward to take bread from a shared loaf and wine/juice from a common cup, while yet other congregations employ serving trays, individual cups, and pre-formed pieces of bread. Some communion services are set to a background of music; others occur in silence. Ordained ministers may or may not preside at the Table, depending on the understandings and traditions of the congregation in question. What remains the same throughout all of these varying Disciples expressions of the Lord's meal is the importance of the Lord's Supper itself and the praying presence of the elder(s).

Most elders know their task is to pray for the communion elements during the service of communion. In some communities this means praying for either the loaf or the cup, while in others it means praying for both all at once. Regardless of such variations, composing and delivering these prayers is often a source of confusion and stress for those in the ministry of eldership. To aid elders in discerning the "right way" to pray, I offer up two different formulas that have come down to us through Disciples tradition.

The first formula comes from a Disciples minister named Russell F. Harrison. Over the course of twelve years, he wrote two different books of elders' prayers. Harrison wrote:

> There is a useful pattern in preparing or writing a communion prayer. These four elements can be your continuing guide:
>
> *Thanksgiving* (to God)
> *Remembrance* (of Jesus)
> *Presence* (of the Holy Spirit)
> *Dedication* (to serve).[11]

This formula will help you as speaker-prayer to compose brief prayers that point to some of the theological meaning(s) attached to the ordinance of communion while also reminding the hearer-prayers of their own participation and responsibilities (service to others and personal devotion through prayer and meditation).

I have included two sets of example prayers from Harrison's work to help you see what a prayer based on this four-fold formula might resemble:

> *Bread:* In joy we come to receive this bread, remembering all that has been done for us that

we might come to this moment of communion. Grant us a fuller sense of the mission and witness to which we have been called. Renew each one in the moments of silence and meditation. Amen.

Cup: For the privilege of taking this communion cup, at the beginning of a new week, we express our deep gratitude, O God. Be with us as we seek a fuller understanding of your will for each one gathered here. Help us to pray not only for ourselves but for one another. Amen.[12]

Bread: As Jesus took the bread and blessed it, we take the loaf in gratitude and thanksgiving today. We come to this table not because we must but because we may. Guide us in our individual silent prayers that each one might know your love and your guiding presence. Amen.

Cup: God of all peoples everywhere, we are grateful to be part of your vast human family across the earth. May the drinking of this cup remind us of our responsibilities which are part of the privilege of being Christian in our day. Amen.[13]

These prayers are obviously quite brief. One of the valuable aspects of Harrison's formula and model for elders' prayers is that while brevity is not the sole goal of a prayer, a great deal can be expressed in a concise manner!

Keith Watkins offers the second formula for elders' prayers at the Table. Watkins did not create this outline. It is a formula he has isolated by reading generations of prayers for the loaf and the cup:

God is named.

Thanksgiving is offered for a blessing that comes from God and for the loaf or the cup.

Bread and wine are mentioned as symbols or emblems of Christ's death on the cross for the redemption of humankind.

A request is made for forgiveness or some other benefit of redemption.

The prayer is concluded in the name of Christ.[14]

For Watkins, this formulaic sort of elders' prayer can be both good and bad. On the one hand, when an elder conscientiously follows this sort of outline to compose a personal prayer, the elder demonstrates a serious respect for Table ministry and an attempt to briefly include all of the meanings and purposes of the Lord's Supper into one prayer.[15] However, an elder ought not feel the need to adhere religiously to any one outline or formula when creating or weaving prayers for the Table. Leaving room for the Spirit to move is just as important as taking prayer at the Table seriously through preparation. Also, because people learn to pray by hearing and observing the prayers of others, it is impotant for elders to "sound like themselves" when they pray at the Table.

Often, questions arise regarding the value of extemporaneous prayer at the Table. Many people are under the impression that extemporaneous prayer is superior to pre-written prayers because it relies on the work of the Spirit and comes more directly from the heart (and is therefore more heartfelt, devotional, and uncontrived!). While I do not counsel against extemporaneous prayer as a genuine and legitimate mode of prayer at the Table, I do caution against elders taking up this form of prayer purely because others have said that it is somehow better. I consider extemporaneous prayer to exist among other spiritual gifts. For some elders, the Spirit is far more likely to inform their study and writing *prior* to a worship experience than to inform their stammering tongue *during* the service! Each elder has gifts from God that are different from the elders with whom he or she serves. Because of this, many modes of prayer and prayer preparation can be used successfully and effectively. The most important thing is that our elders treat their role at the table seriously instead of taking their ministry of Table prayer/service for granted.

Resources for Elders

Published Resources

Keep in mind that while many of these resources are still in print, some of the older works are out of print but may be obtained in many places through inter-library loan if your local library does not have them.

Cartwright, Colbert S. *Candles of Grace: Disciples Worship in Perspective*. St. Louis: Chalice Press, 1992. Cartwright's work consists of a broad examination of Disciples worship. This book is a must-read if you seek to understand the things that are uniquely and/or characteristically "Disciples" in our modern worship services.

Cummins, D. Duane. *A Handbook for Today's Disciples*. Third Edition. St.Louis: Chalice Press, 2003. Cummins's work is a brief, accessible, and engaging introduction to Disciples history, beliefs, structure, and practice. This small book is a helpful overview of the Disciples tradition as a whole and is useful both as a gift to new members and as a "refresher" for elders and longtime members.

France, Dorothy D. *Bless Us, O God: Services and Prayers for Special Days*. Prayers and services for traditional holy days and seasons such as Advent, Ash Wednesday, and Easter are joined by suggestions for more modern special days, such as Week of Prayer for Christian Unity, Reconciliation Mission Sunday, and Earth Stewardship Sunday.

Harrison, Russell F. *Brief Prayers for Bread and Cup*. St. Louis: Bethany Press, 1976; and *More Brief Prayers for Bread and Cup*. St. Louis: CBP Press, 1986. These two pocket-sized books contain a storehouse of brief prayers for loaf and cup. The prayers, in two-to-four sentences, point toward the meaning of the Table and invite the hearer to move into a time of personal prayer and meditation. Although relying entirely on these two volumes is unadvisable, they are quite useful as a starting point for prayer preparation and are also helpful to carry each Sunday in case one is unexpectedly called to serve at the Table with little advance notice!

Morgan, Peter M. *Disciples Eldership: A Quest for Identity and Ministry*. Revised and Expanded Edition. St. Louis: Christian Board of Publication, 2003. Accompanying CD also available. This resource was specifically designed as a course of study for Disciples elders. It contains segments on the history of eldership (both in the New Testament and in the Disciples tradition), the teaching ministry of the elder, the shepherding ministry of the elder, the Table ministry of the elder, and the congregational oversight role of the elder. Each segment has session outlines, suggestions for leaders, work sheets for participants, etc. This resource also comes with a CD that can be used in coordination with some of the lessons.

Shelton, O. L. *The Church Functioning Effectively*. St. Louis: Christian Board of Publication, 1946. Although a bit dated, this resource can be incredibly valuable! Why? Because as you read Shelton's model of church structure and order (committees, subcommittees, and the various divisions of labor within the church), you may very well discover that your congregation still operates this way! If this is the case, this resource will help you to understand how your church functions and from where this model came.

Skinner, Douglas B. *At the Lord's Table: Communion Prayers for All Seasons*. St. Louis: Chalice Press, 2006. Following the advice of Alexander Campbell to steep prayers in scripture, author Douglas Skinner anchors this collection of nearly 200 prayers with biblical references. Prayers for the bread and for the cup are linked with special Sundays, church seasons, hymns, special occasions, and communion themes.

Spry, Marilyn W. *You Are an Elder*. St. Louis: Christian Board of Publication, 1991, pamphlet available for free download from www.chalicepress.com. This pamphlet describes succinctly the role of the elder.

Straub, Gary. *Your Calling as an Elder.* St. Louis: Chalice Press, 2003. Straub's work focuses on the overall call, ministry, and qualifications of the church elder. This work contains helpful and accessible sections that lay out the New Testament qualifications and duties of the elder, modern duties of the elder (which cover a broad range), and suggestions on how to form an elders' circle in your congregation. This book is a short read and could be quite useful as a study guide for any board of elders/elders' circle.

Toulouse, Mark G. *Joined in Discipleship: The Shaping of Contemporary Disciples Identity.* St. Louis: Chalice Press, 1997. This book is a standard text in most Disciples history and polity classes in seminary. If members of your congregation's ministerial staff went to seminary after 1997, chances are good that this is one of the books that influenced their understandings of Disciples tradition. Although parts of the read can be a bit "heavy," this book provides a solid overview of the Disciples tradition that goes beyond Cummins's simpler handbook. If you want to delve deeper into the tradition that has called you into eldership, this a good place to start!

Watkins, Keith. *Celebrate with Thanksgiving: Patterns of Prayer at the Communion Table.* St. Louis: Chalice Press, 1991. This work is both a case study of Disciples observance of the Lord's Supper and an appeal for reform within the denomination. Watkins examines the development of elders' prayers at the Table, points out different trends in the structure of such prayers, and mourns the way that communion prayers have taken on a "diminished character" (see page 23 if you would like to focus on this particular argument). This is a must-read for any elder who is interested in discovering the "right" way to pray at the Table.

Personal Resources

The Ministerial Staff of Your Congregation

A strong relationship with your pastor(s) will enable you to remain accountable in a number of ways. As it particularly applies to service at the Lord's Table, those elders who check in with their minister(s) in the week leading up to a Sunday service tend to be more prepared to lead the congregation into a time of prayer and meditation. If you know the scriptural basis and themes of the sermon on a particular Sunday, your prayer at the Table can weave with the themes of the service in ways that encourage church members to reflect more deeply in their moments of personal prayer.

Conversation with God

One of the greatest resources you have in your storehouse as an elder is your own prayer life. Every minister (ordained or lay) has moments when he or she doubts the call to ministry, feels frustrated with a particular person or situation, or loses a sense of direction. Your personal relationship with God will help to carry you through these periods of strain. Moreover, your own prayer life away from the church can have a very direct effect upon the prayers you share at the Lord's Table. People who are in the habit of talking with God tend to have less anxiety about praying publicly or composing prayers that will later be shared aloud.

Other Elders

Unless you are in the first group of elders called to serve a new church start, chances are very good that you can turn to "elder" elders for help or support. You have been called to minister to your congregation, but you have not been called to serve alone. When elders form warm relationships of accountability and support, all are blessed. Moreover, if you are ever unsure about how to proceed in your role as elder, others among your fellowship of elders may have valuable insights that can help you chart the next portion of your journey in ministry.

Notes

[1]Richard Hamm, Michael Kinnamon, Alvin Jackson, and Sharon Watkins are all relatively well-known leaders within the Christian Church (Disciples of Christ). Richard Hamm was General Minister and President of the denomination during the 1990s, Michael Kinnamon is a major Disciples figure within the ecumenical movement, Alvin Jackson is a well-known Disciples preacher who now pastors Park Avenue Christian Church in New York, and Sharon Watkins has been General Minister and President since July of 2005.

[2]Peter M. Morgan, "Elders, Eldership," in *The Encyclopedia of the Stone-Campbell Movement,* ed. Douglas A. Foster et al. (Grand Rapids: Eerdmans, 2004), 297.

[3]Ibid.

[4]Peter M. Morgan, *Disciples Eldership: A Quest for Identity and Ministry* (St. Louis: Christian Board of Publication, 1983), 22.

[5]Ibid.

[6]Paul M. Blowers and Bruce E. Shields, "Worship: Nineteenth Century," in *The Encyclopedia of the Stone-Campbell Movement,* 788.

[7]Morgan, *Disciples Eldership,* 54.

[8]From "Communion" by the Communication Ministries of the Christian Church (Disciples of Christ) found at: http://www.disciples.org/AbouttheDisciples/Communion/tabid/159/Default.aspx.

[9]Peter Ainslie and H. C. Armstrong, *A Book of Christian Worship: For Voluntary Use Among Disciples of Christ and Other Christians* (Baltimore: Seminary House Press, 1923), 8.

[10]Blowers and Shields, "Worship," 788.

[11]Russell F. Harrison, *More Brief Prayers for Bread and Cup* (St. Louis: CBP Press, 1986), 5.

[12]Russell F. Harrison, *Brief Prayers for Bread and Cup* (St. Louis: Bethany Press, 1976), 27.

[13]Ibid., 53.

[14]Keith Watkins, *Celebrate with Thanksgiving: Patterns of Prayer at the Communion Table* (St. Louis: Chalice Press, 1991), 23.

[15]Ibid.

Bibliography

Ainslie, Peter, and H. C. Armstrong. *A Book of Christian Worship: For Voluntary Use Among Disciples of Christ and Other Christians.* Baltimore: Seminary House Press, 1923.

Blowers, Paul M., and Bruce E. Shields. "Worship: Nineteenth Century," in *The Encyclopedia of the Stone-Campbell Movement,* 768–88. Edited by Douglas A. Foster et al. Grand Rapids: Eerdmans, 2004.

Communication Ministries of the Christian Church (Disciples of Christ). "Communion 2009," www.disciples.org/About the Disciples/Communion/tabid/159/Default.aspx.

Harrison, Russell F. *Brief Prayers for Bread and Cup.* St. Louis: Bethany Press, 1976.

———. *More Brief Prayers for Bread and Cup.* St. Louis: CBP Press, 1986.

Morgan, Peter M. *Disciples Eldership: A Quest for Identity and Ministry.* St. Louis: Christian Board of Publication, 1983.

———. "Elders, Eldership," in *The Encyclopedia of the Stone-Campbell Movement,* 297–99. Edited by Douglas A. Foster et al. Grand Rapids: Eerdmans, 2004.

Watkins, Keith. *Celebrate with Thanksgiving: Patterns of Prayer at the Communion Table.* St.Louis: Chalice Press, 1991.